LAST POEMS

by the same author

POETRY

Possible Laughter (1959)
New and Selected Poems (1983)
Collected Poems (1994)

TRANSLATION

Horace: The Odes (1963)
Catullus: Poems (1969)
Martial: The Epigrams (1972)
La Fontaine: Selected Fables (1979)
Euripides: Helen *translated with Colin Leach* (1981)
Aesop: Fables *illustrated by John Vernon Lord* (1989)
Poems from the Greek Anthology (1990)
Ovid: The Art of Love (1993)
Virgil: The Eclogues (2000)

EDITED WORKS

The Bodley Head Book of Longer
    Short Stories (1974)
The Oxford Book of Short Poems
    edited with P J Kavanagh (1985)
The Folio Golden Treasury (1997)

James Michie

LAST POEMS

OLDIE PUBLICATIONS

First published in 2008
by Oldie Publications Ltd
65 Newman Street, London W1T 3EG
www.theoldie.co.uk

ISBN 978 0 9548176 4 0

A catalogue record for this book
is available from the British Library

Typeset by Hamish Ironside, Weybridge, Surrey
Printed by T J International, Padstow, Cornwall

The paper used for this
book is FSC-certified
and totally chlorine free.

Mixed Sources
Product group from well-managed
forests and other controlled sources
www.fsc.org Cert no. SGS-COC-2482
© 1996 Forest Stewardship Council

Contents

Foreword by Richard Ingrams   ix

En Route

For One Who Thinks I'm Gloomy
    and Godless   1

A Light Dose   2

For D J Enright   3

Obscure Message   4

Greek Island   5

True or False?   6

Cold Comfort   7

Heigh-ho!   8

To my Bearskin   9

Fielding the Question   10

Three Haiku for my Grandsons   11

Memento Mori   12

Travel Pass Photo   13

Double Haiku   14

On Being Fitted with a Pacemaker   15

Loss of Empire   16

Road Rage   17

Ocean View   18

School Speech Day   19

Cross Purposes   20

    21

Jaques' Black Song 22
Piero della Francesco's 'Annunciation' 23
Claude's 'The Enchanted Castle' 24
The Worst of Order, Please 25
76% Proof 26
Wooster and the Modern Muse 27
With Someone in Mind 28
Clancy 29
Lover's Non-Leap 30
Marriage Counsellor 31
Ancient Yoof 32
A Fence Refused 33
Green-Eyed to the Last 34
Damnesia 35
'Dost thou remember Sicily?' 36
No. 46 37
Urbanity 38
Seeing Right Through 39
Freebies of the Future 40
Zero Solemnity 41
The Long Run 42
Unstable Stable 43
Exit, Pursued by a Bear 44
For a Wedding 45
Poe-try 46
Faites Vos Choix 47
The Last Push-Up 48
Thank-You Letter 49
Where Credit's Due 50
Revised Version 51
Awkward Questions 52
A Question of Timing 53
Very Small Point Scored 54
Hide and Seek 55

Warning to All Shipping	56
Value Judgment	57
Solo at Table	58
The Seventh Age	59
For John Michell	60
When I was Young and Easy	61
Alles ist in Ordnung	62
Round Nine	63
Interruptions to an Aphorism of Anthony Powell	64
Quidnunc: Ancient Rome	65
Friendly Fire	66
Collage	67
Crossword	68
For my Half-Sister	69
Summer Dusk: Colquite Cottage	70
Final Union	71
A Salute	72
Striking Midnight	73
Office Nomenclature	74
Homage to Marcus Martialis	75
The Old Actor	76
Tanka	77
Disturbance at Night	78
Self-Help	79
The Birthday Present	80
April	81
Oral Administration	82
À la Mode Zoo	83
Peasant Wisdom	84
For an Extravagant Mourner	85
Nature Notes	86
The Fountain	87
Treble Tanka	88

Dear Mary   89
Is There Nobody Gay in Glamorgan?   90
Deferment   91
Ambiguity   92
Holiday Snapshot: Andros   93
Hate List   94
Love List   95
Chesterfield Replies   96
Post-Mortem Lunch   97
Just a Snook at Auden   98
For Barry Driscoll   99
For a Hypochondriac   100
Talking Against Time   101
Sir Paul Getty's XI v. the Free Foresters   102
Villanelle   103
A Friend in Need   104
Two Haiku   105
When . . .   106
Fine Cuisine Sine Carne   107
Hospital Joke   108
Stoic Announcement   109
Cancer, or the Biter Bit   110

Appendix: James Michie in Conversation   113

Foreword

James Michie began contributing to The Oldie in 1999 and continued to supply a regular monthly poem until shortly before his sad death from throat cancer in October 2007.

James had long-standing links with the magazine, having served briefly as its Literary Editor in the early days when we could afford such a luxury. He was also responsible for one of our most successful features ever, 'I Once Met'.

From the start I had made a rule that The Oldie would not publish poetry, mainly on the grounds that nobody could be bothered to read the flood of submissions that would inevitably ensue.

An exception was made in the case of James Michie for three main reasons. Firstly his poems were quite short. Secondly they were unlike most contemporary poems—perfectly intelligible. And thirdly they were sharp and witty.

I am delighted that we are now able to publish the poems in book form—a posthumous tribute to a remarkable talent.

Richard Ingrams
January 2008

En Route

Poles watched by a boy
From a speeding train,
Too alike, too fast,
The days blur past.

Nose pressed to the pane,
And bothering eyes
Teased by sun and/or rain,
I essay a surmise:

Will the next stop
Be Terminal Lane,
Or a change at last—
Sweet Adlestrop?

Will my next surprise—
If surprise comes again—
Be a shiver of joy
Or a fever of pain?

For One Who Thinks I'm Gloomy and Godless

Since to give thanks is not peculiar
To the religious, out of these sodden skies
I pluck the word 'Hallelujah!'
To jubilate, to bless the surprise
Of survival, the privilege
Of staying afloat in a sea scattered with wrecks.

From the lower decks
I join the ragged cheers
For the hooded calculator on the bridge—
No name, no face, no sex—
The Gizmo that steers.

A Light Dose

Around my skeletal, black-boughed fig
Snowflakes waltz, caper and jig.
A robin balances on a twig,

While I, ancient, infected bard,
Relish the pane-framed, powdered yard,
January's late Christmas card.

It brings back the old boyhood thrill
Of being trivially ill
In my bed under the window-sill.

A happy if not holy ghost,
I take delight in playing host
To a mild germ, with gruel and toast.

For D J Enright

DIED 31ST DECEMBER 2002

Before he could have pricked the hide
Of the gross new year, he died.
     El picador has gone,
     And the brute ramps on.

His smile, like a half-open door,
Invited entry, to explore
     The garden where he grew
     Thrift, honesty and rue.

Honour to Dennis Enright, missed
By all rebels who resist
     Bombast, the pseudo-fact,
     The crass, the inexact.

Obscure Message

Quick, catch my meaning
That floats in between, in
Between my last joke
And blue cigar smoke.

Listen now, hear
With your innermost ear
What I'm trying to say
In my unstated way.

Perpend. Please attend
To your ancient friend
Whose stare into space
Is a search for your face.

Greek Island

Two dolphins half a mile away
Umlaut the blue vowel of our bay
And conjugate the verb to play.

Hoi polloi, elsewhere, take their fun
More seriously. Museums are 'done'—
And so are they: the turnspit sun

Grills them in thousands on the beach
Kebab-like. Out of hearing's reach
Mermaids are groaning, each to each.

True or False?

I bald, she grey, we met—was it again?—
Drinking atrocious corporate champagne.
She had good eyes. After some vapid chatter
She, suddenly: 'Look, it doesn't really matter,
But did we once, in the Sixties, sleep together?'
You could have knocked me down with the old feather.
'You must remember that old men forget,
Especially veterans of the Chelsea set.'
'My memory's hopeless, too.' Rocked by amnesia,
We held hands, which made the rest much easier.

Cold Comfort

Mock, Muse, the latest tourist hero,
The man who holidays sub-zero,
Who brings to the Antarctic zone
Condoms, cuff-links, telephone,
Who, goggled, on his snowmobile
Ogles a penguin, snaps a seal,
Whose rations (unlike Cherry-Garrard's)
Were purchased on account at Harrods.
Muse, mock him merrily: he's not
Remotely linked with Captain Scott,
He's the new grockle who will soon
Play table tennis on the moon.

Heigh-ho!

(WITH ACKNOWLEDGMENTS TO BELLOC)

My days of global worrying are long gone.
I'm now a joker calloused by the years.
When people badger me to comment on
Aids, clones, the ozone layer, nuclear fears . . .
I simply wag my great big furry ears.

Deplorable, I know, but there you are.
As the arrival of the unthinkable nears—
Atomic chaos, a colliding star,
Calamitous climatic change—my dears,
I simply wag my great big furry ears.

I'm part of it, so I can sympathise
With a world drenched in blood and sweat and tears,
And yet I somehow lack the enterprise
To act: I watch, reach for the glass that cheers—
And simply wag my great big furry ears.

To my Bearskin

I like dead pets the best—and, Bruin,
You're my ideal, a gorgeous ruin
Whose fulvous pelt and claws and head
Exoticise my Willesden bed
Where, winter-happy, underneath
Your harmless snarl and futile teeth
I sleep without one twinge of guilt
At making you my ursine quilt.
I scorn political correction:
You're mine by natural selection.

Fielding the Question

'Love two women equally?
How can that possibly be?'
'Well, old son,
It's often and easily done.
There's moon up there and a sun,
And though I'm lunar at heart, being Cancer,
When it comes to naked heat
Moonbathing simply can't compete.
How's that for an answer?'

Three Haiku for my Grandsons

You're on stage! As Lear,
Hotspur, Bottom, Trinculo—
Who knows? But act well.

Don't look for justice,
Sentenced already to bear
The load of our hopes.

Life's a tough exam:
Not all pass it. Whereas death's
A doddle—you can't fail.

Memento Mori

Old Body gives a better
Prognosis than old Mind does.
Unfailingly we get our
    Sharp reminders.

Aches, coughs in the morning,
Dizziness, cardiac hop,
Served like bills, are a warning:
    Time must stop.

We fore-enact our death
In every staircase fall,
And guess by laboured breath
    At none at all.

Mirror previews a skull
Skeletally stark,
While eyes, growing dull,
    Rehearse the dark.

Yet Mind, silly old dog
Who can't read 'House for Sale',
Continues still to flog
    His waggish tail.

Travel Pass Photo

This mugshot shows a stumblebum,
    A smuggled refugee,
A psychopath . . . There must be some
    Mistake—it can't be me.

That hangdog look, those puffy eyes,
    The untrustworthy face . . .
The camera that never lies
    Malfunctioned in this case.

Double Haiku

'Idle'—of all words
The idlest. I spend two-thirds
Of each blessed day

Fossicking on spec
In old mines. Time's a blank cheque
I fill in my way.

On Being Fitted with a Pacemaker

What with sex and fags and liquor,
Silly old mulish heart,
Dear unregenerate ticker,
You needed a kick start.

Hey presto! It was done.
Now with my magic inner
Supplementary volt,
Though I'll never be a winner
And can't pass as a colt,
I feel a new urge to run—
For buses, even for fun.

Loss of Empire

First, rumours of barbarian migration
(Premonitory fibrillation);
Then the hordes approach to the borders
(Bowel disorders)
And the camp fires whose blaze all night is
Gastroenteritis:
Next the revolt of provinces, betrayal
By governors, old friends (senses begin to fail);
Finally the cardiac assault on Rome,
The capital you vainly christened James,
Pride, headquarters, home.
When your world is burning
Will you, like Nero, be learning
A new tune on the fiddle among the flames?

Road Rage

When old friends fall off the perch
I've an impulse to complain:
Damn you, why have you left me in the lurch?
Then I think again:
No. I'm pottering along in my jalopy
And I've been passed by a sleek black car
Going somewhere thrillingly fast and far
In the wrong lane.
Why feel stroppy?

Ocean View

To sit in an old Panama hat
On the quayside staring at the view,
As Mediterranean grandfathers do,
Looks tranquil, halcyon. But the case
Is not always that.
Waves can be hostile, fidgety bores
Unless you match their restlessness with yours.
Make love, make money, make mischief to the end,
Or you may have to face
A sea that is not your friend.

School Speech Day

WITH SON AND SUNDERED MOTHER

In the modernistic chapel
　　Uptight, itching on my chair
(Sunbeams mischievously dapple
　　Benedictine skulls or hair),
I hear 'ethos', 'heaven', 'achievements',
'New appointments', 'sad bereavements',
And again inertly grapple
　　With the paradox of prayer.

At long last, release, euphoria,
　　And—what I can share—
A picnic purchased at Victoria
　　Plus a good Sancerre:
Perched above immaculate fairways,
Underneath unvirgin airways,
Three—a trinity. Deo gloria—
　　And, for a day, a pair.

Cross Purposes

'My dear, you know I'm fond of you . . .' 'Yes.
I know. I'm fond of you. What's wrong?'
'It's just that it's been so. . .' 'I can guess.
Difficult living with King Kong?
Something about togetherness?'
'Just that it's been so very long
Since . . . ' 'What? I changed the baby's nappy?
I'll do it from now on, make you happy.

Why don't you let me teach you chess?'
'It isn't any of those things.
It's more a sort of homelessness
I feel at home. When the doorbell rings
I wonder, is this my address?
Here nobody but the budgie sings . . .'
'Songs? Now we're talking. Okey-dokey,
Tonight let's go to the karaoke!'

Jaques' Black Song

All the world's a fair,
   Pitched on an unfair ground.
The big wheel, jammed, is there,
   And the sad merry-go-round.

The palmist brings no luck,
   The trampoline's a flop,
The coconuts are stuck,
   Or milkless if they drop.

You're handed featherless darts
   To aim at a numberless board,
Then conned by the bogus arts
   Of eating fire or a sword.

The clowns are far from funny,
   The slot machines are bent.
This morning you had money.
   Now it's all spent.

The mermaid in her booth
   Was the biggest swiz of all,
And the only show of truth
   The crazy mirrors hall.

Piero della Francesco's 'Annunciation'

Is there a distant, solitary flute
Jubilating? No, silence is absolute.
Like a raised baton the Corinthian column
Prohibits sound. Beween them lies a solemn
Awkwardness, an area of unease:
The angel's searching for his speech, and she's
Braced for the news—is it good or bad?—she's
In grave doubt. One word only, and let
The hidden flute breathe for the hidden boy!
This is the nanosecond before joy.
Aloft, the Alchemist, with a faint smile,
Transmutes the lead of history in His phial.

Claude's 'The Enchanted Castle'

What a paradise for a honeymoon,
You might think—beside a northern sea
A southern palace, Lord Cupid's private place,
Wild but not lonely, as the few deer
And faint yachts attest. Who wouldn't be happy here?
The answer in this case
Is Psyche, newly arrived. Soon,
A casualty of the old collision
Between imagination and reality,
She will try to drown herself.

                              Enchanted, the eye flits
From bough to bough, lights on the parapet,
Hovers over water, but is always drawn
Back to the girl who sits
Slumped in prevision
Of the end of love, and watches the sun set
As her woes dawn.

The Worst of Order, Please

As focus scatters and ideas peter,
My rooms become, in desperation, neater.
But matchboxes, jugs, seashells, all aligned,
Can't give the lie to my chaotic mind,
And the exotic fruit and vivid flowers
Merely contradict the colour of the hours.
Would it were the reverse case:
It, not me, all over the place.

76% Proof

Here, I thought, I sit,
A contented man, children happy, work not yet done.
I'm not bored,
I love a woman, I'm still semi-frisky
In the sack, I have friends. Then the sun
Went over the yard-arm and I poured
A treble whisky,
Which proved the opposite.

Wooster and the Modern Muse

(THE MUSE ENTERS THROUGH THE FRENCH WINDOWS)

'What ho! I mean all hail, Muse!
I feel pretty lyrical today. What shall I sing?
As that Virgil chappie used to say.'
'The modern subject is often the nearest thing.'
'But that's a pair of old suede shoes—
Dashed unpoetic.'
'You could meditate upon that mustard-pot.'
'Absoballylutely not!'
'Well, then, it's up to you to choose.'
'What about some blithe thrush warbling on a lilac
        spray?'
'Pathetic! Lilac? It's long past May.
You must be joking.
And you won't see a single thrush in Woking.'

'Muse, you're a toad.
I was just launched on a humdinger of an ode —
And you sank it.
O Muse, you're a wet blanket.
I need a drop of inspiration. Jeeves!'
(Purse-lipped, the Muse leaves.)

With Someone in Mind

'I do not love thee, Dr Fell . . .'
I know that feeling very well:
However, I don't have the same
Block as the poet (Brown by name)
When it comes to giving reasons why.
Take two: at once they multiply
And breed like fruitflies, until I
Have sixty-four of them, to tell
Why I detest sight, sound and smell
Of the unlovable Dr Fell.

Clancy

Irishman, bibliophile, raconteur, master cook,
Loner, old soldier, ex-crook,
Clancy was my flatmate for four years
Of good talk and no tears.
One day I said, 'Well, old friend,
Let us consider the end.
You know the routine if I'm the first to die,
But suppose you go under a bus,
What do I do? Who are your next of kin?'
The typical reply
Was accompanied by his gap-toothed grin:
'Just don't make any fuss.'
So I left it at that.
A fortnight later he fell flat,
Instantaneously dead,
In the Museum of Transport, thus
Achieving a pun on what I'd said.
Three months he lay on the slab, no kin found
To put him decently underground—
He had no money and not much underwear—
And we were all ready to pass round the hat,
When a billionaire
(The names Clancy dropped weren't often winners),
To whom all thanks and glory,
Paid for a grand funeral. Happy ending to the story.
May we rest in peace, all of us small sinners.

Lover's Non-Leap

Once I begged you, but you thought no
   (Maybe I thought no too).
Now you say yes and I don't know,
   Like you then, what to do.
If I were Rochester I'd go
   Straight for the simple screw.

When it comes to leaping into bed
   Nothing matters except
The right when, and the unsaid—
   And so we've never leapt.
If I were Hardy I might shed
   Tears 'ruefully bewept'.

Marriage Counsellor

I was reckoned a 'sound' adviser
    On other people's lives.
But am I any the wiser
    After my several wives?

One may rage like Baudelaire
    At peasant saws, yet they're true.
'He who is born square
    Will not die round'—that's you.

Yes, once I was an oracle,
    A pilot, a sage Greek;
Now I paddle my coracle
    Up Shit Creek.

Ancient Yoof

On my desk, gathering dust
Is an alabaster bust
Bought at a country fair
And marked *Horace*—a beardless Roman youth
Of about seventeen
With a supercilious air
Quite unlike the imagined man I once translated.
Last night in the firelight he seemed to wink
And I thought I heard him say, 'So you think
I'm the poet? Well, I'm not. I'm his son
(I bet you never knew he'd fathered one),
And if you want the truth,
I loathed his crappy odes. The Golden Mean?
I never mess with Mister In-Between.
"It's great to die for your country"? Hopelessly dated.
"Keep your balance when the going gets tough"?
That sort of stuff
Went out with Cato. But one thing he wrote was okay:
Carpe diem. Have a nice day!'

A Fence Refused

Hup! Hup!
My old cock-horse, why can't you get it up
Tonight? What's wrong?
Only last Tuesday you were on song—
A model of a veteran performer.
Have I become a mere bed-warmer?
Old hack, I guess you're tired.
Like everything else I thought I owned,
You were only hired.

Green-Eyed to the Last

Jet underwear, opal skin,
Legs just so, eyes bound blind,
Half dressed to kill, or be killed,
Victrix or victim, fervently free-willed,
My darling was greedy for her mortal sin,
Which was uncommitted, for I couldn't get it in;
Nor could I get it out (of my mind)
That another old, more boring man
Does and can.

Damnesia

In minimal landslides memory goes—
It's like trying to touch your nose
When you're drunk, and you can't find it.
When it begins, you don't much mind it—
What does it matter, the name of a book or a play,
Or whether it was the day before yesterday
Or last Thursday? But soon
You can't remember where you went on your
    honeymoon
Or which year it was. When it ends,
You forget the names of old friends
And your own telephone number. But stop fretting
When your retrieval system starts to go rotten.
Just try to remember this: it's better to do
    the forgetting
Than be the one forgotten.

'Dost thou remember Sicily?'

(OSCAR WILDE)

Yes. I do—in the days when, apart from the slap
Of waves, the yap
Of a stray mongrel, the cough of a goat
Or the chug of a solitary motor-boat,
Mediterranean islands
Rhymed meaningfully with silence.
Now the bays are stitched up by water-skiers,
Airport music follows you into the trattorias,
The alleys are choked with Vespas, and backpacking
    wankers,
While out in the overfished sea enormous tankers
Loom.
Big sky and ocean—but there seems no room
For an old-fashioned man.
Next year I plan
To investigate
The chillier charms of Porlock or Harrogate.

No. 46

'I wished to share the transport—oh! with whom?'
Groaned Wordsworth, and I understand his gloom.
Today I shared it with a mobile phoner,
Six foul-mouthed schoolgirls blowing bubblegum,
A backpacker who'd lost his money, the owner
Of a smelly dog, a Caribbean bum
So comprehensive it took up two places,
A youth with a plastic shovel aiming junk
Food at his mouth, somebody making faces
Which weren't funny, and an Irish drunk.
Not another Englishman—except the driver,
A Mr Toad who wouldn't change my fiver.

Urbanity

Christmas, flu, an unpromising dawn:
Then I saw a dogfox cross my lawn.
I gaped through glass, my vulgar 'Coo!'
Cancelled in favour of 'How do you do?'

Seeing Right Through

Once you reach seventy, the wise advise,
View everything as a blessing in disguise.
The snag is, with my eyes, at this late date,
Disguises are damned hard to penetrate.

Freebies of the Future

The rain-resistant afternoon
(Staged by the Government) ends. Next show
(Gratis) will be a cute little moon
And London's chemical sunset glow.

Citizenship! Togetherness!
Chauffeured (no charge) towards my rus
In urbe (rent-controlled), I bless
Us idlers on the dawdling bus.

We drones contribute to the hive.
Our lack of zeal adds Wooster zest
To chips with everything. I thrive
(State-funded) in the warless West.

Zero Solemnity

A*****, the people's Poet Laureate, trying
To boost his income and revive his dying
Inspiration, cobbled up a 'Hail
Millennium' poem for the *Sunday Mail.*
One day, extracorporeally—just think!—
He soared to the heavens from his kitchen sink.
Appalled, Apollo read it, and glanced down:
'Manikin, cease your motions. Cede the crown.
Your bays and nose alike are turning brown.'

The Long Run

As we've failed to make futuroscopes,
We live uneasily with the years—
Millions, nuclear-free, one hopes,
Or just a few decades, one fears.
How long, O Lord, how long? No lens
Can foresee Homo sapiens.

Long after Everest has become
A dump of rusted mountain cars
And Norfolk a morass, will some
Amused historian on Mars
Grant us a footnote? Will our race
Be well reviewed in outer space?

And who, once we've dropped out, will win
The Darwinian marathon? New germs?
The cockroach or the terrapin?
Or those slow-moving pachyderms,
Predators like us, our old pre-daters,
Crocodiles and alligators?

Unstable Stable

Three nags have screwed me up. My vet,
Quite early on, put down Regret.
Later the same death sentence
Was handed down to old Repentance.
Which leaves Remorse.
Now there's a living nightmare of a horse!

Exit, Pursued by a Bear

You'd think by now that the Great Grizzly in question
Through over-eating might have indigestion.
But he ravens on in the chase.
As I dodge through the bad lands
Of old age, I drop behind me baits of honey,
Notes of repentance, promissory money,
Lies, jokes—all useless. When we come face to face,
I shall probably offer to shake hands;
But he'll insist on the full embrace.

For a Wedding

Cooks in the night kitchen, bake
A rich, a rococo cake
To signify the combination Annie-and-Jake.

By the big Cornish tide
Jubilate, flutes, and slide,
Trombones, to match the harmony of groom and bride.

Strum, shift that thumb,
Guitarist, cuff that drum,
Percussion man—this is an epithalamium!

New daughter, old son,
You've heard the starting gun
For an endurable marathon. Now run and run.

Poe-try

It was dank and dismal December,
The leaves they were ragged and rent,
As I poked at the ultimate ember
Of my fire in the borough of Brent,
The dolorous borough of Brent
Where my days are immutably spent,
Trying in vain to remember
The name of one desperately dear
Who was once my good angel here.

I longed for some sweet swan of Avon
To carol a phrase of good cheer
To counter the gloom of this year,
This doom-laden dog of a year,
But my eye caught the eye of the raven
Opening his ebon beak,
But before the old groaner could speak
His detestable, dreary, absurd,
His trisyllabical word,
I strangled the bird.

Faites Vos Choix

One of the casualties of age is
Possibility—jobs, sports, holidays, lovers.
The options narrow to which shoes to wear, which
Cheese to buy, which pages
To turn for an hour (once it was four). One discovers
The minimalisation of choice.
Shall I at last tackle that difficult Joyce,
Reread an old favourite, or begin a
Controversial Booker Prize winner?
The answer's a foregone conclusion.
Freedom becomes what it never seemed before:
    illusion.

The Last Push-Up

These days both gut and brain thinkers
Seem to prefer cremation,
But daily my feelings harden
Against the combination of crude clinkers
And refined oration.
I've come, almost warmly, to terms
With the cold clods and the dank worms.
Bury me in my garden.
And though as a gardener I was famously lazy
I'll do my best to cultivate one daisy.

Thank-You Letter

FOR CHARLES SPRAWSON

A man who hangs your picture
And then gives you lunch
Deserves a gentle stricture,
At least a friendly punch.

But since that can't be sent
Via our parcel post
I name your punishment—
Dinner, you guest, me host.

We'll open the file marked 'Sports':
Long-skirted volleying women,
Wingers in baggy shorts,
And Esther Williams swimming;

And those never to be forgotten
Moments which mist the eye—
Carnoustie tamed by Cotton,
Prince Obolensky's try . . .

Where Credit's Due

It's easy to make sons,
Much harder to make men:
So the French proverb runs.
Verb. sap. Does that mean, then,

That proud parents should preen
Themselves, rather than bless
The lucky maverick gene
Of an ancestor? Well, yes.

For if their likely lad
Turns out a criminal creature,
The world will say, 'That was bad
Nurture, no fault of nature.'

Revised Version

One cries, 'Repent! Prepare to meet
Your Maker!' to an empty street.
Another croons, 'God does the job'
And draws a happy-clappy mob.

Awkward Questions

I breathe, but do I properly live?
I have, but how much do I give?
I eat and drink and laugh all right—
Habit mimicking appetite?
Worry is everywhere: I am
Concerned, but do I care a damn?
I'm sitting on a solid chair,
But am I, is it, really there?
Such questions, food for thought too late,
Shelved, mouldy, past their chew-by date,
Accumulate, accumulate.

A Question of Timing

Last year old Jeff, who lived above me, died.
Soon afterwards a hearse drew up outside
And two men, top-hatted and black-frocked,
Knocked.
'It's not me you want', I cried.
Funereal embarrassment: wrong door,
Wrong man. This year I'm not so sure.

Very Small Point Scored

'Look,' I cried, 'at that copper beech
Against the blue of the sky!
Doesn't it, almost, answer the question why?'
But my old duchess said, 'Why do you always preach
About nature? It's a topic
Which, being myopic,
You can't really know much about.
Aren't you being a tiny bit pretentious?'
Stalled in self-doubt
(I don't know the difference between
A broad and a French bean),
I rallied pedantically: 'My dear, you meant "sententious".'

Hide and Seek

When your glasses aren't to be found
And you can't track down your brolly
And your keys are lost, you're bound
To suspect you're off your trolley.

Too right. One's on your nose,
The other's in the stand;
As for the door-keys, those
Are hiding in your hand.

Warning to All Shipping

FOR HALF A DOZEN SEMBLABLES ET FRÈRES

Hide! Jump overboard! Take to the boats!
Here comes the Monster of the Anecdotes,
The *Titanic*-sinker. Glitteringly he floats

Into the Gulf Stream of our common room
To drift among us. Drift? He's planning whom
To scupper with his conversational doom.

The Queen, the Quorn, the Quality, the war in
Qwertyuiop—don't try to put an oar in
Or you'll catch a crab, he's bumping *and* he's boring.

Preambling, rambling, rabbiting, reminiscing,
When old men begin telling and stop kissing,
Must this be how we plug the gap that's missing?

I dreamed of a mountain, at the top a sage:
I'd climbed to ask him what to do about age.
He answered, 'Speak less. Simply turn the page.'

Value Judgment

Is one exquisite Sung bowl
More precious than a squalid soul?
Could you let that drunk old geezer
Die, to preserve the Mona Lisa?
Put imponderables in the scales—
Ethics wobble, balance fails.
Ticklish questions such as these
Must be resolved by deities.
The answers human beings give
Only show they like to live.

Solo at Table

I eat to live who lived to eat.
Daily I calibrate and heat
Fodder to fuel my idle sins
With calories and vitamins.

Input, methodically chewed,
Meals half-enjoyed in solitude
Nutritionally suffice of course,
But dialogue is your only sauce.

I feel the prick of appetite,
Most of my teeth are there to bite,
But where's the missing *belle artiste*
Who makes me raven like a beast?

The Seventh Age

Old men turn into actors, one-dimensional,
Typecast. Each studies and perfects his part
Sedulously (it's only unintentional
In the case of the drunkard or the silly old fart).

It would be supernumerary to mention all
The roles they specialise in, but for a start
There's the old soldier, the sly dog, the sage,
The dread nostalgist (où sont les neiges?),

The hypochondriac, the reminiscer,
The lounge lizard with the flickering tongue,
The hearty shoulder-squeezer and cheek-kisser,
The stickleback who opts to swim among

Minnows, and that egregious target-misser,
The spry impersonator of the young.
There's only one role that comes anywhere near
The truth, but don't attempt it—it's King Lear.

For John Michell

I seldom risk a smile these days,
    My teeth being stained with smoke;
But still, occasionally, I raise
    A rictus at a joke.

I'd like to leave as Cheshire cats
    Vanish—amused, in style.
A grin without a mouth? Yes, that's
    Old Plato's perfect smile.

When I was Young and Easy

That bird's zigzag across the air
Is the signature of a drunk millionaire
On a blank cheque. The sky bulges
With blue luck and a south breeze indulges
Fantastical hopes
Of windfalls in white envelopes.
At one o'clock Allegra comes to lunch
And my satyr's hunch
Is that we'll amplify our afternoon
With a crescendo. *And* it's a full moon.
Flick the roulette wheel, let it spin
Any old way,
Today
I fancy myself to win.

Alles ist in Ordnung

He declared a great war on mess.
Dust was anathema, drunkenness
Verboten, bills punctually paid,
Shoes polished, letters filed, beds made.
At the end of a lifelong fight
He was in control of everything in sight,
Borders defined, chaos in mad retreat.
The landscape grinned. His world was neat
Barring the corpses. Victory or defeat?

Round Nine

The Ref insists, 'Box on.'
And so, eyes closed, wind gone,
He squares up again to Fate,
That nebulous heavyweight,
The ghost with the hammer in his hands,
Who now lands
Another uppercut. My God, that hurt!
Stay upright, keep alert,
The mind begs, but the old legs implore
Honourable accommodation on the floor.

Interruptions to an Aphorism of Anthony Powell

'In the end most things in life'
(*A stillborn child? A lunatic wife?*)
'—Perhaps all things—'
(*Outrageous fortune's arrows, slings?*)
'Turn out to be appropriate.'
(*That's not the mot juste, mate.*)

Quidnunc: *Ancient Rome*

I'm just back from a Bay of Naples cruise.
So what's the latest news?
Who won the chariot race—the Reds or the Blues?
Did the blond gladiator from Thrace really lose
To the dwarf netman from Syracuse?
What do you think of the new built-up shoes?
Is it true that Manlius has taken to sporting Gallic trews?
Where can I scrounge a free lunch with booze?
Who's who, this month? Or rather, who's whose?
Are the bread shops still besieged by queues?
Have you seen the blind juggler from Toulouse?
Strangled, you say? And no bruise?
No motive? No clues?
J'accuse!
It's all the work of those pestilential Jews.
(Thank you for your aid with the rhymes, O Muse!)

Friendly Fire

The Scotch—what a verminous race!
Canny, pushy, chippy, they're all over the place,
Battening off us with false bonhomie,
Polluting our stock, undermining our economy.
Down with sandy hair and knobbly knees!
Suppress the tartan dwarves and the Wee Frees!
Ban the kilt, the skean-dhu and the sporran
As provocatively, offensively foreign!
It's time Hadrian's Wall was refortified
To pen them in a ghetto on the other side.
I would go further. The nation
Deserves not merely isolation
But comprehensive extermination.
We must not flinch from the final solution.
(I await legal prosecution.)

Collage

(BEING 14 SENTENCES CULLED FROM POSTCARDS
RECEIVED OVER THE YEARS)

The ears are rather poignant.
Why has no one given Stephen Spender a drink?
I look forward to painting you.
The child you bounced on your knee has written a
    very, very boring book.
My hands are worse this winter.
I'm as happy as a clam.
What is Holman Hunt up to here?
Keep, poet, those erotic visions of yours.
The comforts of philosophy are only for the strong.
How kind of you to respond so promptly.
I love you.
The Bering Sea is hellish swimming.
Mein Gott! Women!

Crossword

Ivory tower or padded cell?
Magic square or tortoise shell?
For me it is the bathysphere
In which I can descend and peer
At a sea-world where wonders swim—
The homophone, the acronym
And the rare nonce-word. Puns in shoals
Wriggle, anagrams writhe in holes,
Tropes glitter, ambiguities glide
Elusive, unidentified,
Like mermen, and archaisms lurk
Half-invisible in the murk
Like coelacanths.
                You want a clue?
Fish in the unconscious (2).

For my Half-Sister

Margaret Mary is dead.
At bad moments, usually, the less said
The better; nevertheless
I, who am too old to express
Sorrow in tears, shed
My due invisibly.
              To me
Long ago you were kind, and to three
Daughters a valiant mother
Whom they have cause to bless.
On my own, slower way to bed
I sign this wreath 'Your brother'.

Summer Dusk: Colquite Cottage

The river rightly applauds itself
All day and night by a green shelf
Of grass (platform for dancing lambs);
And where a snag of rocks half dams
The current and the water talks
Loudest our warden heron walks,
While overhead top-secret trees
Communicate fresh mysteries
In leafy code. A stir of sheep,
A single chirr or hoot or cheep:
Otherwise silence. Now for sleep,
In which this ancient Cornish stream
Will wander through my Xanadu dream.

Final Union

Once I wasn't, but now I am
My best friend. The lion and the lamb
Lie down together, the primeval
Tyrannosaurus rex beside the civil
Pet, unanimous, agreed
On what to eat, which books to read,
How to travel and where to go
For amusement. Daily we say hello—
Not a word more, thank God—and nightly
Snore companionably tightly.
There's no need to be neatly dressed
Or shaved or sober. Who would have guessed
That at the end of a fractious life
I'd find myself—the perfect wife!

A Salute

Gentlemen, I propose a toast
To KO Peppiatt, that most
Uncelebrated man. No mere
Bank clerk, he was the Chief Cashier
Of the Treasury, the chap who wrote
His signature on every note
With such panache that we all knew
Sterling was sound, his promise true.
That's seventy years ago. The new
Fellow's called Merlyn Lowther, a name
That doesn't quite suggest the same
Authority and gravitas.
So, gentlemen, please raise a glass
To that forgotten hero, that
Monument-worthy bureaucrat—
Kenneth Oswald Peppiatt!

Striking Midnight

Go gentle into that good night,
I say contrarily. Just go,
For if you kick and yell and fight
You'll only stage a horrorshow.

Better to fade like an old clock
That, wheezing, summons one last chime,
Then with a minimum of shock
Stop bothering to tell the time.

Office Nomenclature

His job description was 'Administrator',
At fifty pounds a day.
He failed. Now titled 'Chief Facilitator',
He gets even less pay.

Homage to Marcus Martialis

Whenever we meet we soon reduce
Each other to silence. It's no use,
Since you bore me and I bore you,
Attempting small talk as we do.
The exchange is like a game of squash
Played in a court with walls of plush—
No sound, rebound. We grunt, compete
In speechlessness, and share defeat.

The Old Actor

I loved the lighting and the clothes—
Green jerkins or bluejeanery—
I loved a hunchback, a false nose,
I loved the change of scenery,

I loved my deep bows, the applause,
The fans, the glitz, the glam.
The only part I hated was
The man I really am.

Tanka

FOR CHRISTINE YAU

Bread riots by ducks,
Picnic with raised umbrellas,
Tombstones, rainbow shared.
Thank you. Rarely is calm found
In the world hurricane's eye.

Disturbance at Night

Fireworks or gunshot? We learnt next day
When they carted the shoeless corpses away,
When the goggled outriders, the colonels in gold braid
And unearned medals, the motorcade
Klaxoned past, and the band played
'Fraternité' after the fratricide,
And again it was time to hide.

Self-Help

When the brain races
But minutes crawl,
When fungoid faces
Sprout from the wall,

When your last dream
Was of Lear's heath
And tomorrows seem
Waste of breath,

When at four o'clock
You hang on the brink,
It's time to take stock:
Be your own shrink.

The Birthday Present

This lot is orthoclase feldspar
Defined by the geologist,
But, in my dictionary, here are
Eleven moonstones for your wrist.

April

The spring was sprung,
The grass was riz
When I was young,
When was was is.

But now the spring
Don't spring because,
Though birdies sing,
The is is was.

Oral Administration

Daily, Corsodil for my molars
And, for my heart, those Indian bowlers
Adizem and Ramipril.
There's also one large vitamin pill,
Warfarin for prevent a clot,
Senokot for you guess what,
ICaps, which my oculist
Swears will delay impending mist,
Plus Bendroflumethiazide
For God knows what. Joking aside,
Am I a man, or doomed to be a
Zombie, a walking pharmacopeia?

À la Mode Zoo

A narcissistic bitch, who'll always choose
Disastrously, except when buying shoes;
An affable horned goat, whose doom was sealed
The moment that his wedding bells had pealed;
A blind beaver, also a bad chooser,
Destructive in defeat, a rotten loser;
A nanny and a Filipina maid,
One overworked, the other underpaid;
And last—a detail that I almost missed—
A yapping dog that sees an analyst.
What a grotesque, umbrella-worthy shower!
Hogarth, thou shouldst be living at this hour!

Peasant Wisdom

'The name of the game on the moon is play cool'
Were the words of the astronaut Aldridge. Fool!
The name of the game is, wherever you are,
Don't reach for the moon, just stick to your star.

For an Extravagant Mourner

Dear man, when feelingly you speak
Of loss, pain, despair,
Pause; for you are not unique:
We have all been there.

Her illness, to your cost you know,
Was irreversible, fatal.
But grief's not a disease, and so
For that be glad a little.

Would your old friend approve the sight
Of you sorrow-destroyed?
Respectfully I suggest she might
Be posthumously annoyed.

Nature Notes

I

The spry jerboa, had he shoes,
Would scorn to put them on his feet,
Although that is the place to choose
If one is trying to be neat.

He'd stuff them with old cabbage leaves
Or dump them in the nearest pond.
No rodent seriously believes
In bounds one may not go beyond.

II

A politician when disgraced
Might crawl away and hide, you'd think;
Yet spiderlike, flushed down the waste,
He clambers back into the sink.

The Fountain

FOR THE CHELSEA ARTS CLUB

Cupid, lord of our lily pool,
With your admiring frog
And the wee jet that plays it cool
In the parched days of the dog,

Dear young-old boy threatening the sky
With no arrow to your bow,
Whose aim is gloriously high,
Whose score banally low,

Long may you stand on your conch shelf
And spout and dribble and, thus,
Repeating endlessly yourself,
Parody some of us.

Treble Tanka

'Why do all parents
Tell children the same old lie—
"You're loved equally"—
When it's clear they have favourites?'
Anthony asked his grandad.

'Ah,' said the old man
(He was fond of saying 'Ah'),
'It's not quite a lie,
It's half the truth. The most loved
Is often not the best loved.

Do you follow my meaning?'
'No,' said Anthony, 'I don't.'
'But you will one day.'
'Grandad, I think you're crazy.'
'Ah, that's why you're my favourite!'

Dear Mary

Dear Mary,
I have a problem for you—and it's pretty hairy.
Recently a man I'd never seen before
Without so much as a by-your-leave walked through
    my front door,
Ensconced himself in my favourite chair,
Helped himself to a cigar, poured a whisky,
And with an intolerably familiar air,
Before I'd scarcely drawn breath,
Announced, 'I'm an old friend, don't you remember
    me?—
Charlie Death.
I'm staying with you officially, from now on.'
That was a month ago, and he still hasn't gone.
He shares my bed, borrows my shoes,
Peers over my shoulder at the daily news,
Monopolises the loo, and fills in the crossword clues.
Mary, I'm so mortified
I've even thought of committing suicide.
But since that wouldn't be, any more than he is,
    very nice,
Please, please give me your advice.
What is the most correct, the politest, the best
Way to get rid of this pestiferous, unwanted 'guest'?

Is There Nobody Gay in Glamorgan?

'Is there nobody gay in Glamorgan?'
Was the minuscule wail on the wall,
And my heart and the sensitive organ
I dangled were moved by this scrawl.
Is there not one good man in the county,
I thought, from here to Worms Head,
Who out of mere bisexual bounty
Could take the poor bugger to bed?

Or mightn't some dating computer
Or dial-a-pal telephone find
A compatible person to suit a
Lost cause in the back of behind?
Then I saw (as I gave it a final
Shake in the manner of males),
Even lower case on the urinal:
'There's nobody gay in all Wales!'

Deferment

Old age
No good:
Silly rage,
Vapid food,

Too much drink
Without being drunk.
Can't think.
No spunk.

Love still there,
Children, friends,
But less to share
At both ends.

Time to go.
Make a move!
Can't, though,
Stuck in groove,

And too unpleasant
To say goodbye.
For the present,
Won't die.

Ambiguity

'Why do people keep going?'
Larkin asked. There's no knowing
Exactly what he meant.
Out of his life, I presume,
Away from his jazz-stale room
To Stoke-on-Trent or Tashkent
Or wherever they went.
Or did he mean, 'Why
Do people keep going
When they could so easily choose to die?'

Holiday Snapshot: Andros

Below our balconied flat
A quince, a palm, groves of bamboo,
Four goats, a cast-off shoe,
Blue jeans motionless on a line,
And on a whitewashed wall a black cat
Mediterraneanly supine,
Like sleeping you.
And that, in Greek, is that.

Hate List

Misprints, clocked socks, spiders, red-top papers,
Hydrangeas, hamburgers, mathematics, capers,
Saunas, waiting-rooms, hamsters, cheap umbrellas,
Auctions, window-shopping, doorstep sellers,
Gardening, beach reading, Canova's 'Three Graces',
Messing about in boats, flat treeless places,
Breakfast in bed, anchovies, Wagner, rap,
Community singing, motor racing, Jap
Cuisine, whodunnits, an illegible letter,
Princess Diana . . . There, I feel much better.

Love List

Kedgeree, anagrams, tulips, waterfalls,
The jack of clubs, mail-boxes in old walls,
Owls, ammonites, orchards, witch-hazel, giraffes,
Scotch Roman type, graveyards and epitaphs,
Eating alone in restaurants, chiming clocks,
Tangos, applewood fires, Spätlese hocks,
A night sleeper, a Horatian ode,
Beachcomber, an Arcadia by Claude,
A balcony over a river, amethysts,
Hot chestnuts, a Havana, making lists.

Chesterfield Replies

'You wrote maxims, my Lord, on how to live.
Now that you're dead, have you one more to give?'
'Ghosts become none the wiser. My advice
Remains the same: in every sense be nice.'
'So what's your final message from the grave
For the next generation, sir?' 'Behave
Civilly.' 'That's a vague prescription. Let's
Be more precise.' 'Very well then, pay your debts.'
'But what about the mystery of Love?'
'Follow your nose—and my remarks above.'

Post-Mortem Lunch

After the funeral I chose to go
To an almost empty restaurant in Soho,
Where I thought I saw, through rain-distorted glass,
Corpses in clothes gesticulate and pass,
Macintoshed zombies. I was seized with dread:
Was I, too, one of the programmed dead?
The answer came with my Mongolian lamb
(With lemon zest): I eat, therefore I am.

Just a Snook at Auden

Died at the frontier mulberry-faced Fletcher,
History master, hater of future,
Failed to confront the bleak ultimatum
     Issued by autumn.

This death rejoices life, releases
The manacled smiles, the cramped neuroses,
Makes the dwarf taller, the wimp fitter,
     The stammerer utter

His first aria under the glacier.
Now larks fly higher, roses grow rosier;
Awaiting a new school of moorland hikers
     Marvellous acres.

For Barry Driscoll

After he died
I had a queer conceit
That things as well as we suffered distress:
The bottle mortified
To be only half drunk, his feet
Sorely missed by his shoes, an unread book
With a miserable, disappointed look.
Pathetic fallacies, I know.
Even so
I hear his jokes like puppies masterless
Whining for play in a world he worked to bless.

For a Hypochondriac

Blood pressure: fine. Coagulation:
Neither too thin nor yet too thick.
Pacemaker: works. Some consolation
To know you'll die in perfect nick!

Talking Against Time

Dear Vladimir—or may I call you Didi?—
I'm being informal not because we're seedy,
Or smell, or wear disreputable boots,
But to mark the years we've been in deep cahoots
To kill time in this draughty, trainless station
With any class of decent conversation.
We fire at the old enemy not with guns
But reminiscences, quotations, puns.
At dawn, counting the corpses of the hours,
We crow like cocks and think the day is ours.
Some hope! And yet, though Pyrrhic in the end,
Victories are still victories, old friend.

Sir Paul Getty's XI v. the Free Foresters

In this oval dingle
Skill vies with luck
(J G Cake sneaks a single,
Gatting caught for a duck!)

And a kestrel hovers
In a pewter sky
Over the overs,
Bored. Whereas I,

Earthbound, geriatric,
Myopic, enjoy
A six or a hat-trick
With the zest of a boy,

Till the lithe slow bowler
With a feint of his wrist
Fools the stiff stonewaller—
And we're all dismissed.

Villanelle

Here's old December like a shabby vet
Come to put down a hunting dog that's ill.
Am I resigned to the needle? No, not yet.

Or call me an aged fruit-tree, not a pet,
Whose leaves are running out of chlorophyll,
Fit for chopping and burning. No, not yet.

I might have time to place one final bet,
Write one more decent poem, draft a will.
Packed, ready for departure? No, not yet.

I know how the contract reads: 'The sun must set
And darkness follow afterwards', but still
I long to add the rider: 'No, not yet.'

I've an obscure feeling there's a debt—
To whom? For what?—still owing, and a bill
Clamouring to be settled. No, not yet.

Why can't I leave the feast without regret?
I've gormandised and swigged and fucked my fill.
Here's old December like a shabby vet.
Am I resigned to the needle? No, not yet.

A Friend in Need

FOR P J

A bad night for dreaming:
Snakes and vertigo.
Mauve, yellow, in coils of gunge
They erupted from the wallpaper.
Next, silently screaming,
Halfway up a skyscraper
I watched a mastodon plunge
Bellowing five hundred feet
Splat onto concrete.
Horrorshow!
Then someone changed the reel and
You turned up in a tractor
With briar pipe and tweed cap—
Inveterate actor—
And we crossed grassy New Zealand.
Thank you, old chap.

Two Haiku

FOR A TEENAGER

Is this it—real love?
I can't tell. My jury's still
Out. Please, a verdict.

FOR AN OLDIE

Was it love—or fraud?
Long ago your twelve brought in
'As guilty as hell.'

When . . .

When grass grows grey
And mouths don't mean
The words they say
And the future has been,

When jokes don't work
And nor can you,
When you're bored by the Turk
and sick of the Jew,

When you've lost the beat
Of the drums of advance,
Rediscover your feet,
Invent a dance.

Fine Cuisine Sine Carne

FOR DROGO

I used to be shy of the stove
But cooking is now my chief love.
 I've converted to food
 That's green and is good
At persuading the bowels to move.

I only have dealings with gas
(Electricity is a faux pas).
 You should taste my boiled sprouts,
 Broad beans and mange-touts!
I'm twice the performer I was.

Believe you me, it's no sweat.
All you need is a pan and some heat.
 You don't need much nous
 To stir-fry couscous,
And vegetable cutlets are great.

Hospital Joke

Shelley had his little whine
—The 'superincumbent hours'—
Mine is life without weather and wine,
Nothing but slops and flowers.

The moral of this verse is:
However dire one's ills,
Be thankful for small nurses
And blue remembered pills.

Stoic Announcement

Strike it lucky or strike it catastrophic,
There's no excuse for not being philosophic.
The customer's bound in honour to rejoice,
Hack or Hyperion, in Hobson's choice.

Cancer, or the Biter Bit

I used to fancy crabmeat as a treat:
Now Crab's the epicure, and I'm the meat.

Appendix

James Michie in Conversation
with Hamish Ironside

The following interview took place at James Michie's home in Kensal Rise, London, in February 2001. A longer version was published in P N Review 140 (volume 27, number 6, July–August 2001).

HAMISH IRONSIDE: How did you begin writing?

JAMES MICHIE: One of the things that interests me is why some people become writers, especially writers of poetry. It seems that, quite early, you are gripped by words as if they were not notional means of communication but as if they had some talismanic quality in themselves. I used to read, at the age of ten, dictionaries. For pleasure. If I found a new word like 'pyrope', I would get a kick out of that! What is it in somebody's genes, what peculiarity, that makes you think that words are that important? Why do they matter so passionately in the decorative or non-utilitarian sense? I then started writing poetry at ten or eleven—ludicrous stuff, needless to say; it doesn't matter.

One would write some post-Keatsian nonsense in one's head, and then I remember getting up at school at fourteen and going down to the classroom and writing it down before I went to sleep again, for fear I should lose it.

Your education continued at Oxford University, where your contemporaries included Philip Larkin and Kingsley Amis. I wonder whether their work was influencing your own?

Well, I did read Kingsley's poems as he wrote them because he showed them to me, and back then he was tremendously influenced by Auden, as I was. So I would say, if you can spot some influences, which is always fine, that Auden would be the greatest influence. As he must have been to a lot of people of my generation. Maybe particular sorts of ways of thinking do create a feeling of sameness. Not sameness, but anyway recognition.

Perhaps you tend not to be influenced by your contemporaries, but you and your contemporaries react to the same things, or are influenced by the same things?

I just think one is always influenced, whatever that word means, by the greatest poets of one's century. Yeats and Auden, MacNeice, Frost—it doesn't matter. Somewhere underneath my poems, whether you can spot it or not, there's a little nod to one of these people sometimes. But that's the point about originality: there's no such thing as total originality. I'd add Dylan Thomas—a poet I don't unreservedly admire, but certainly he wrote some great poems. To any poet, what people are doing with language at a particular moment is always fascinating, and so you are bound to be influenced. If it shows too much, it is a failure, because you're imitating rather than using the poet as a springboard. But if it doesn't show, it's still there; it must be there. Auden was one of the first people to promote the idea that comic poetry was as exciting poetically, and demanded exactly the same skills as serious poetry. Although he didn't write a lot of comic poetry himself, he was responsible for taking comic poetry seriously, he recognised that it can give you the same Housmaniac shiver, of 'this is the real thing beautifully done', as a love poem or an elegy. The fact that they're making you laugh is just as valid as the fact that somebody else is trying to make you cry.

One of the things I like about your Collected Poems is that it's about the right thickness: 128 pages. I don't know whether you wrote a great many more and not many of them got in, or whether this was simply a product of having spent a long time before you said a poem was finished.

I think there were twenty years in my life—I'm not counting exactly—when I didn't write any poetry. I associate it with the fact that it was a period of responsibility—a job, a family—and I hate to admit it, but I think that for some people writing poetry is essentially an anarchic thing. I think whatever enabled me to write poetry was not connected with whatever enabled me to be responsible as a human being, and I much prefer to be the latter. And so it's only rather late in my life—when one's responsibilities are, naturally, just as large, but they appear less—that I started again.

So you stopped because of the moral element?

Well, these aren't conscious decisions, they're unconscious or subconscious decisions. I didn't say 'I'm not going to write poetry' because of course I wanted to write poetry. But I think it's true to say that exercising other elements of my personality in a good direction was inimical to poetry. The history of poets is littered with early deaths, suicides, drunkenness . . . why? There are so many. I do think there is something morbid about writing a poem. It's an annoying thing to admit, but in my experience there's some truth in it.

And necessarily so? It comes with the territory?

I don't know, maybe not for other people; I never think that somebody like Roy Fuller felt the pull between writing poetry and whatever else he was doing. He just had two lives and they didn't interfere with each other. But in my case I did feel obscurely that there was a tug of responsibility, and the poetry went. It came back, as most things come back, up the sink or through the back door. You could be seized by the desire to write a poem—there's a slight equivalent to an epileptic fit. When you're going to write a poem you can feel it coming on; you feel nervously excited, and then you have to be alone, and then you have to get as much down as you can when it's hot, and in the light of dawn you can see whether there's the making of a poem there.

I think most poets can tell you the same sort of story: it either comes out almost right in an extraordinary and unexpected rush, or the thing sits there for several weeks, on the table, until you get it right. I've thrown away very few poems since what might be called juvenilia. I tend to sort of worry them like a bone—it's pretty rarely that I tear it up and say it'll never come right. Maybe because one is determined to record whatever experience or mixture of experiences prompted the poem. You don't want to lose it.

Like Auden, you are a rhymer.

I prefer rhymed verse. I think the difficulty is . . . you might almost say that rhymes are running out. A poem that I admire—Vikram Seth's 'The Golden Gate'—is a piece of intricate and skilful rhyming, which also manages to convey extreme casualness. To rhyme and to seem casual—you can't at any point suspect that the man wrote 'bird' because he'd written 'word' four lines before—is an achievement! There are one or two poems which don't have rhymes, but I write in rhyme because it meets that desire to make a shape. Sometimes I think the desire to make a shape—almost like a potter—is the genesis of a poem. I must have written one or two poems in which I didn't have any subject to write about, I wasn't moved emotionally by a particular event or sight, but I saw a poem in my head, like a shape. I wanted to write a certain sort of poem—I could almost describe things like 'it should have a hard top, a soft middle . . .'

Right, but here we're not talking about a visual shape on the page, we're talking about a musical shape.

We're talking about a musical shape, and yet it involved things like what to do with consonance and syllables, before I'd even thought of what I was going to write about. And then I'd wait for this empty vessel to fill up, with some trivial or tragic event, which would enable me at last to use the shape I'd dreamt months before. I don't know whether anybody else would say that—but shape often comes first. Life isn't short of emotions, but you have to find, sometimes, emotions to fit the shape.

My impression is that most people don't do that now, but generally start with finding a subject—rather than treating the poem as a fairly musical production.

Well, it's a question of ear. Not all poetry is about music, or concerned with it. I know a very good poet who can't write a limerick. You just have to say 'how do you do it?' Obviously, he's got a tin ear in one respect, and probably he doesn't go in for sound effects; nevertheless, what he says is so good and so well said that it stands up as excellent poetry. Other poets, you can say, are musical—somebody like Milton, you are always aware of music.